Beads & Wire

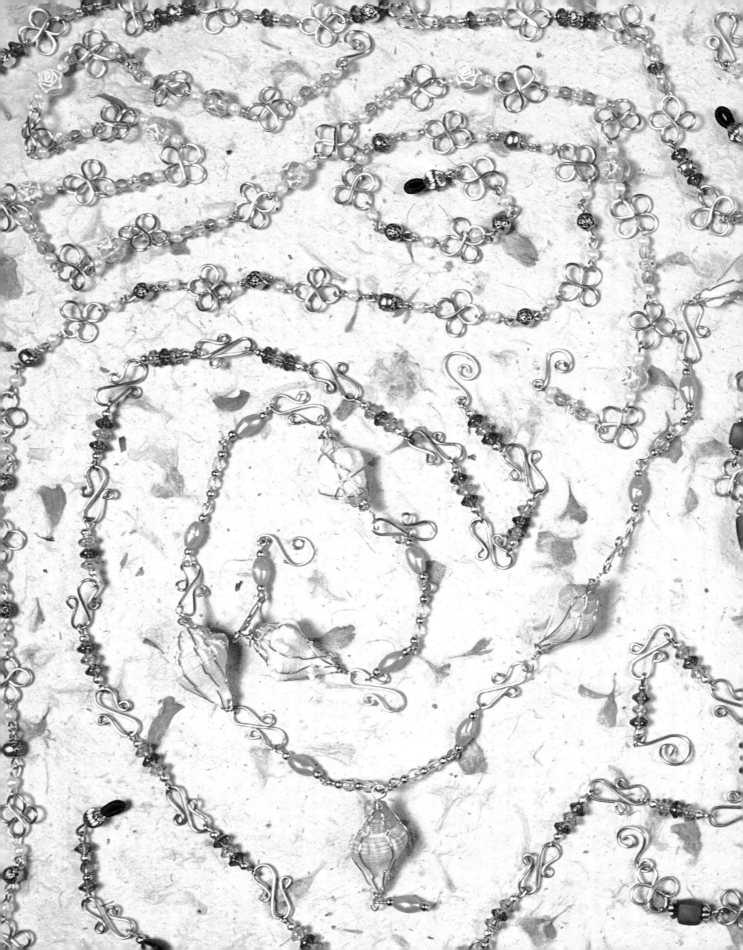

Beads & Wire

Carolyn Schulz

SEARCH PRESS

First published in Great Britain 2001

Search Press Limited
Wellwood, North Farm Road,
Tunbridge Wells, Kent TN2 3DR

Reprinted 2002

ISBN 0 85532 975 0

Suppliers

All materials used in this book were
supplied by The Beadery®, who
manufacture beads in Rhode Island,
USA. If you have difficulty in obtaining
any of the materials and equipment
mentioned in the book, then please
visit the Search Press website for details
of suppliers: www.searchpress.com

Alternatively, you can write to the
Publishers at the address above, for a
current list of stockists, which includes
firms who operate a mail-order service.

*I would like to dedicate this book to all my friends at The Beadery®
and to Al Seifert, who is responsible for getting me involved in the
creative craft industry and making a hobby become not just a career
but a way of life.*

Acknowledgments

It has been my great privilege to work with the design team at The Beadery®
when working on this book. Together with Mimi Huszer Fagnant,
Lorraine Kazan and Heather MacDonald, I believe we have come up with a
wonderful selection of projects to inspire readers to experiment with beads
and wire. Thank you all for sharing your ideas and designs, and for teaching
me your techniques. Thank you also to Chris Servidio, Steve Lord and
Scott Seifert, who gave us the time and resources to experiment.

It has been such great fun to work with the team at Search Press. I have
appreciated the professionalism as well as the encouragement and support.
I particularly enjoyed the three days of photography with Sophie, Tamsin
and Lotti. It truly was a pleasure and I thank you so much.

Publishers' note

All the step-by-step photographs in this book feature the author,
Carolyn Schulz, demonstrating how to make pieces using beads and wire.
No models have been used.

Contents

Introduction

Beads have charmed and fascinated men, women and children throughout the ages. They have been used as symbols of wealth and power, to barter for food and land, and have held religious importance as well as being enjoyed simply for their beauty. Perhaps it's the endless variety of shape, colour, texture, size and materials which accounts for the appeal that beads have for all ages and races of people.

For many years I have held the belief that everyone has a creative side to their personality which, when allowed to surface, can provide the individual with so much more than just a completed project to enhance their wardrobe or decorate their home.

The ability to make something which reflects our personality and gives notice of our own unique style is reason enough to indulge in crafts, but beyond that, it is now recognised by medical practitioners throughout the world that the satisfaction of creating something with our hands has a tremendous therapeutic value. When we share this creative activity with friends or family, the benefits are obvious in the reinforcement of those bonds of friendship and love which 'make the world go round'.

With this in mind, I am constantly on the look-out for new techniques and materials which will create new project designs to fill my home and share with loved ones. Not surprisingly, the latest trends combining beads and wire struck me with their uniqueness and simple beauty. As a lover of beads, I was delighted with yet another new way in which to use the marvellous collection of beads I had been saving for 'just the right project'. As I began experimenting, I could hardly contain the thrill that overcame me when I started to realise the endless possibilities of how one could use and combine various bead and wire techniques, both old and new.

This book offers the reader a wide variety of different projects, along with variations in colour and theme to inspire further ideas and encourage experimentation. We have included something for everyone, from trendy jewellery to exquisite decorated vases. There are stylish wedding accessories, sophisticated place settings, unusual Christmas tree decorations, wind chimes, decorated pots and more.

So if you're looking for a new technique or a new look, get creative with beads and wire!

Toast the bride and groom with these exquisitely unique wedding goblets.

Materials

I love to mix different materials, mediums and techniques when I experiment with projects. I found it fascinating to see the different textures and effects that emerged when combining various beads and wire and placing them on different backgrounds such as skin, hair, glass, terracotta, paint, paint effects, fabric, trees and light!

Beads themselves come in almost every conceivable shape and size and in a range of colours and finishes. There are round, faceted, flower, oval and textured beads and more. They come in matt, frosted, pearlised and metallised finishes to name just a few.

Wire is available in different colours, strengths and gauges. For projects needing a structure that will hold its shape, use the lower gauges (around 18); for flexibility and a more delicate look, use the higher gauges (around 28).

The tools most often used are inexpensive jewellers' long-nosed and round-nosed pliers, wire cutters and scissors.

For the painted projects in this book I used acrylic paint applied using a sponge brush (a natural brush could be substituted), and a natural sponge. Acrylic varnish was also used. To twist wire I used the handle of a wooden spoon. For measuring you will need a ruler and tape measure.
You will need a variety of rings, findings, cords, shells, ribbon, braids, elastic and fishing line, which are attached in various ways including silicone glue and other adhesives, all of which are itemised under the appropriate project. A cocktail stick can be used for applying tiny drops of glue.

Don't be restricted to using exactly the same materials that I have used. Experiment with different colours and sizes. Substitute materials that are to hand. Enjoy the satisfaction of creating something that is uniquely yours.

These optional tools (right) have recently become available. The wire straightener uses its padded flat nose to take all the kinks out of wire. The three-in-one tool was designed by The Beadery® to combine the flat sides of the long-nosed pliers, the round-nosed pliers and wire cutters all in one tool!

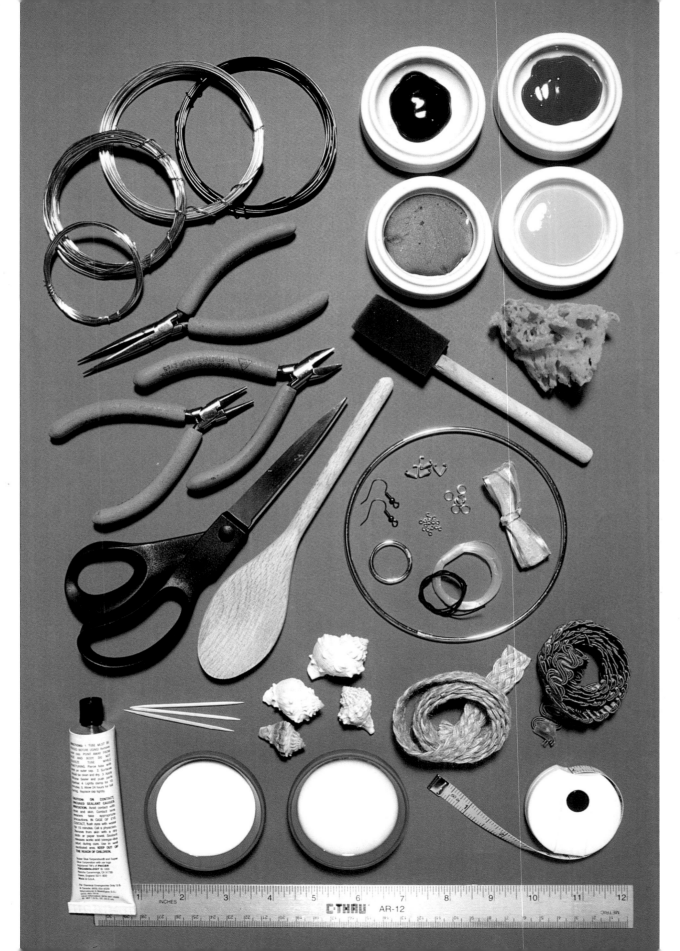

Necklace, earrings & bracelet

The following steps show how easy it is to make a fashionable jewellery ensemble using four-loop wire flower links interspersed with round pearlised beads. The necklace and bracelet are made up of the required number of flower and bead links (which can be altered to suit the length required), with a hook clasp attached to each end. To make the earrings, you can attach one bead link and one flower link to each earring finding, or choose a combination to suit you.

You will need

18 gauge black wire
6mm (¼in) round beads:
  10 black pearl lustre
  12 grey pearl lustre
Fish hook earring findings
Wire cutters
Long-nosed pliers
Round-nosed pliers
Ruler

Flower link

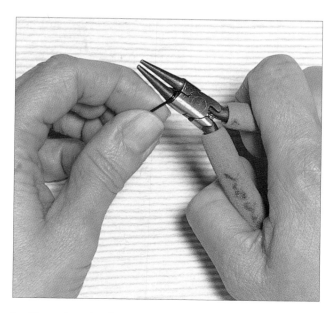

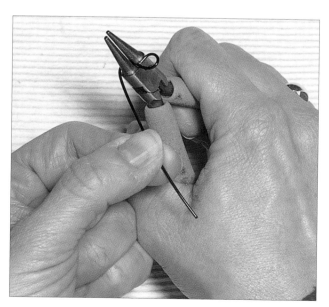

1. Cut a length of wire 8.5cm (3¼in) long with wire cutters, and form a loop at one end by twisting the wire around one jaw of your round-nosed pliers.

2. Make a second loop in the same way, opposite the first one.

10

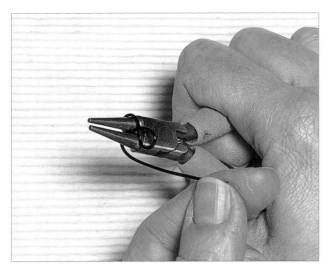

3. Move one jaw of the pliers back into the first loop. Now make a third loop between and below the first two loops.

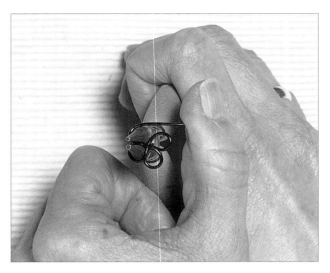

4. Move the other jaw of the pliers into the first loop. Now finish the flower link by making a fourth loop opposite the third one.

5. Trim off the excess wire with wire cutters.

6. The finished flower link.

Bead link

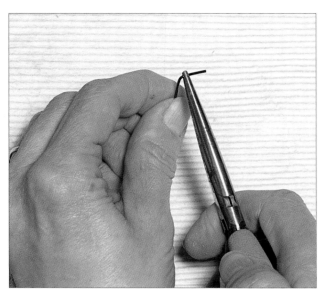

1. Cut a 3cm (1¼in) length of wire and using long-nosed pliers, bend it at right angles, 9mm (½in) from the end.

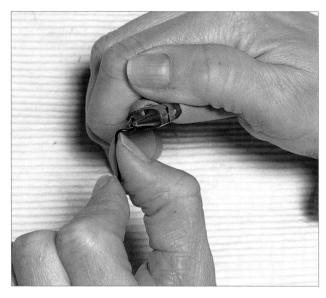

2. Roll the wire back on itself around one jaw of the round-nosed pliers, to make a loop.

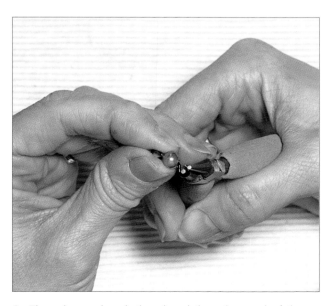

3. Thread on a bead, then bend the other end of the wire in the same way as in step 1 and repeat 2 to form a second loop.

The finished bead link.

Hook clasp

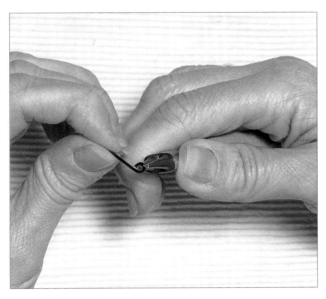

1. Cut a length of wire 4.4cm (1 ¾in) long and form a simple loop at one end with round-nosed pliers.

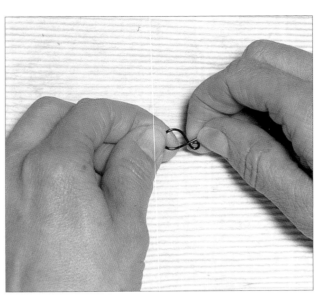

2. Use your thumb to curve the wire round in a large loop, so that the end comes back to the small loop.

3. Use round-nosed pliers to curl the end inwards to make a spiral.

The finished hook clasp.

Assembly

Once you have made flower links, bead links and hook clasps, you can assemble the various parts into necklaces, bracelets or earrings, using the following techniques.

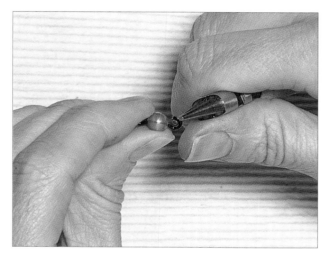

1. Open one loop of a bead link using round-nosed pliers.

2. Insert the loop through either a flower link or hook clasp loop. Both are shown. Close the bead link loop using long-nosed pliers.

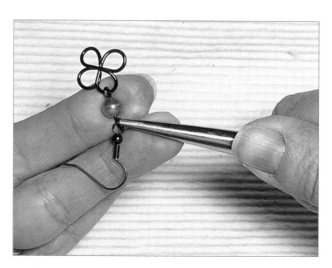

3. The bead link can be attached to a fish hook earring finding in the same way, to make an earring.

Necklace

This is made using two hook clasps, fifteen flower links and fourteen bead links – seven made with black pearl lustre beads and seven with grey pearl lustre beads.

Bracelet

This is made using two hook clasps, seven flower links and six bead links, three made with black pearl lustre beads and three with grey pearl lustre beads.

Earrings

Each earring is made using a fish hook earring finding, one bead link and one flower link.

By experimenting with different colours of wire, formed in a variety of simple shapes and combined with beads of varying colour, shape, size and texture, you can create unique, stylish jewellery. You might also want to consider making chains for glasses or sunglasses by attaching your wire and bead link chain to spectacle holder findings; or a belt, just by making a longer chain.

Hair band

Stylish hair bands that appeal to sophisticated young adults as well as those of discerning maturer years can be created by simply weaving beads onto wire. You could also wire a single unit, or a cluster of units, to a hair slide, clip or comb.

You will need

3m (11½ft) 24 gauge silver wire

160 black faceted 4mm (⅛in) beads

2 black 9 x 6mm (⅜ x ¼in) oval beads

Black elastic

Wire cutters

Long-nosed pliers

Round-nosed pliers

Ruler

PVA glue and cocktail stick

Scissors

1. Cut two pieces of wire 137cm (54in) long. Hold them together and 5cm (2in) from one end, twist them together with your fingers for 13mm (½in).

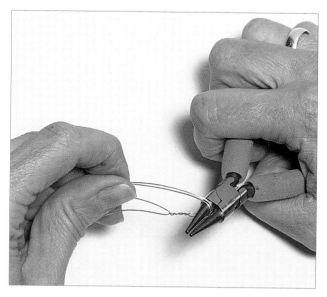

2. Take the two 5cm ends and form a loop around the round-nosed pliers.

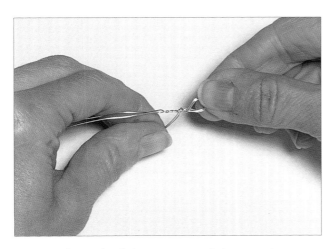

3. Wrap the ends of the wire around the twisted section at the base of the loop. Trim off any excess with wire cutters.

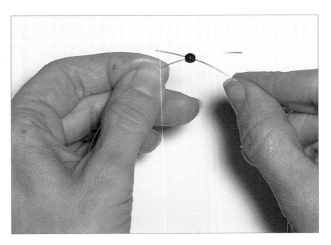

4. Pull the wires apart, then take a faceted bead and thread the top wire down through the bead and the bottom wire up. Push the bead right to the bottom of the wires, near the loop.

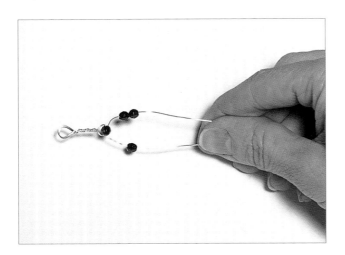

5. Thread two beads on to the top wire and one bead onto the bottom wire.

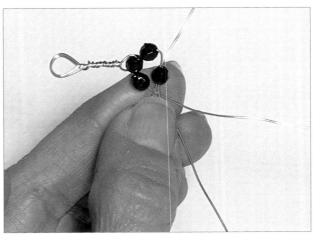

6. Pull the second top bead downwards and thread the bottom wire up through the hole to form a cluster.

7. Measure 5mm (¼in) along the bottom wire and thread on four beads. Pull the wire around, thread it up through the first bead and pull tight to form a second cluster.

8. Repeat step 7 with the top wire.

9. Measure down 5mm (¼in) along each wire and repeat steps 4, 5 and 6 to create a central bead cluster. Next repeat steps 7 and 8 to create two more bead clusters.

10. Continue repeating steps 4–9 until you have completed the hair band, finishing with a central cluster of beads. Take the ends of the wire and twist them together as in step 1. Repeat steps 2 and 3.

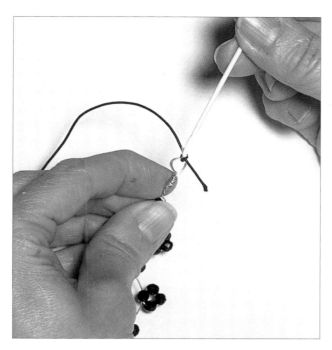

12. Thread one oval bead on to the elastic and pull the loose end of the elastic back through the bead. Slide the bead over the glued knot to secure. Thread on the second oval bead and repeat steps 11 and 12 to secure the elastic to the other end of the hair band.

11. Measure the required length of elastic. Tie one end to the loop of the hair band with a reef knot and place a tiny drop of glue over the knot, using a cocktail stick.

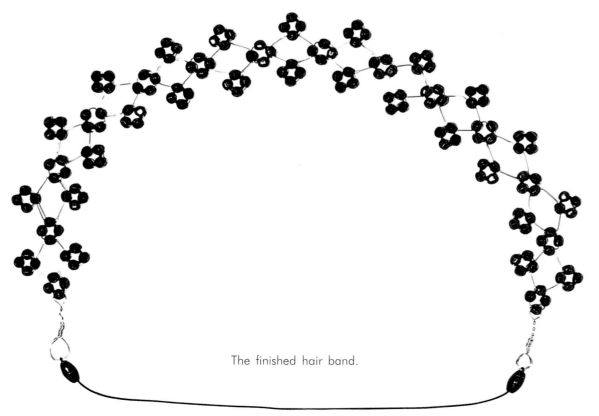

The finished hair band.

Dark-coloured beads such as these jet-like faceted beads complement fair or red hair.

Place setting

For a more substantial wire base that is still flexible, you need only twist two wires together, which in itself produces a pleasing textural effect. By decorating this base with delicate flower and leaf beads in pretty pearlised colours, you can create an attractive piece which is remininscent of a garden vine creeping up a trellis.

You will need

- 24 gauge silver wire
- 18 gauge silver wire
- 6mm (¼in) round beads in pearl lustre colours (blue, green, dark rose)
- 4mm (⅛in) faceted beads in dark amethyst
- 4mm (⅛in) round beads in pearl lustre turquoise, dark rose
- Dogwood flower bead, blue
- Dogwood leaf bead, green
- Starflower bead in blue, green
- Wire cutters
- Wooden spoon
- Long-nosed pliers

1. Cut a 1 metre (39½in) length of 18 gauge wire and fold it around a support such as a chair back or bannister rail.

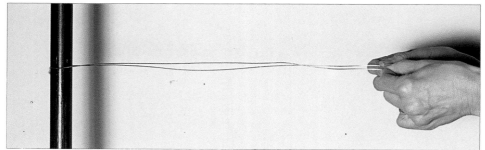

2. Twist the ends of the wire around the handle of a wooden spoon. Twist the spoon until a taut twisted cord is formed. Use wire cutters to cut the twisted wire away from the support and the wooden spoon. Trim both ends to create a 31cm (12¼in) length of twisted cord.

3. Using long-nosed pliers, form a flat curl at one end of the cord.

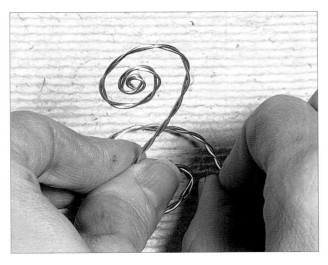

4. By hand, form a coiled base for the place setting to stand on. Pull it into a tighter coil as you go. Make a small loop at the end to finish off the sharp edge.

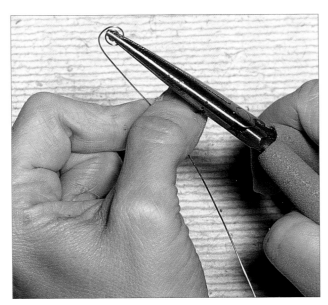

5. Cut a 30cm (12in) length of 24 gauge wire and form at curl at one end, using long-nosed pliers.

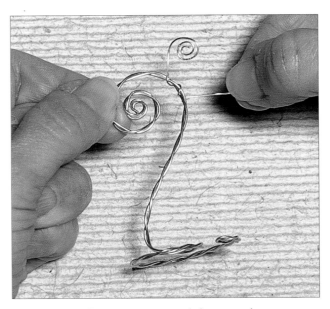

6. Wrap this thinner wire around the twisted wire cord twice.

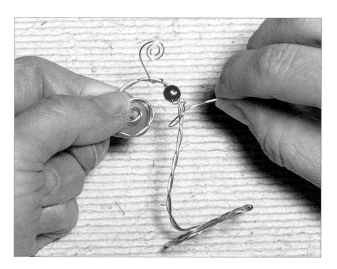

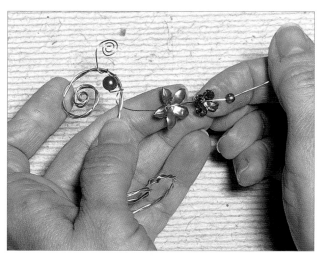

7. Thread a bead on to the thin wire and wrap it around the cord twice more.

8. Thread a green starflower bead, then a blue dogwood flower bead and finally a 4mm bead on to the thin wire.

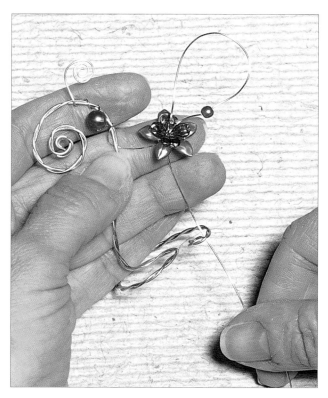

9. Pass the thin wire back down through the blue and green flower beads but not the round bead, and wrap it twice around the twisted cord.

10. Thread a second round bead, another colour, on to the thin wire and then twist the wire twice around the cord.

11. Thread a single leaf bead on to the thin wire and pass the wire around through the leaf bead again. Repeat with a second leaf bead.

12. Wrap the thin wire twice round the twisted cord.

13. Thread a blue starflower then a 4mm bead on to the wire. Pass the wire back through the flower bead and position over the top of the leaf beads from steps 11 and 12. Wrap the thin wire twice round the cord.

14. Trim off all but about 5cm (2in) of thin wire with wire cutters. Form a curl with the remaining wire using long-nosed pliers, to finish off the piece with a flourish.

Co-ordinate a whole table setting with this delicate floral design. For the serviette rings, candlesticks and stemmed glassware decoration, simply take the 31cm (12in) length of twisted cord from step 2 and form a small curl as in step 3. Decorate the length of the twisted cord with thin wire threaded with flower, leaf and round beads in a repetitive pattern, following steps 7–14. Wrap or twist the decorated twisted cord around the napkin, candlestick, stemmed glass or vase.

Wind chimes

Create this beautiful garden or conservatory feature by mixing elegant faceted beads with real, natural seashells. The beads are strung on to clear fishing line for an ethereal effect, while delicate gold wire wrapped around the shells brings out their unique shape and texture. Fifteen bead and shell chimes are attached to a metal ring, and when hung outside, they produce a delicate tinkling sound in the breeze.

You will need

24 gauge wire
13cm (5in) metal ring
2.5cm (1in) metal ring
Fishing line (monofilament)
Crimp beads
Beads:
  4mm (¹⁄₈in) peach faceted
  4mm (¹⁄₈in) peach pearl lustre round
  4mm (¹⁄₈in) faceted rose quartz
  4mm (¹⁄₈in) pink pearl lustre round

4mm (¹⁄₈in) gold round
6mm (¹⁄₄in) deep pink rondelle
10 x 7mm (³⁄₈in x ¹⁄₄in) peach squatty bicone
13 x 6mm (¹⁄₂in x ¹⁄₄in) peach elongated bicone
Wire cutters
Long-nosed pliers
Round-nosed pliers
Ruler
Scissors

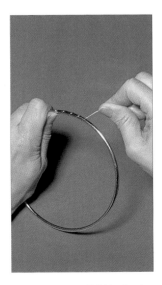

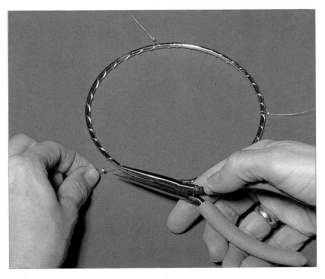

1. Wrap 1m (39½in) of wire around the 13cm (5in) metal ring, with the twists about 5mm (¼in) apart. This will help to keep the hanging chimes evenly spaced.

2. Cut three 46cm (18in) pieces of fishing line, using scissors. Thread one piece through a crimp bead, around the metal ring and back through the same crimp bead. Use pliers to pinch the crimp bead very hard to crush it. This secures it in place. Trim the excess fishing line. Repeat with the other two pieces of fishing line, spacing them evenly around the ring.

3. Add a second crimp bead to the first piece of fishing line, about 3cm (1¼in) from the metal ring, and pinch to secure. Add the beads as shown. Complete by pinching a crimp bead at the end, to secure the beads in place. Repeat with the other two pieces of fishing line.

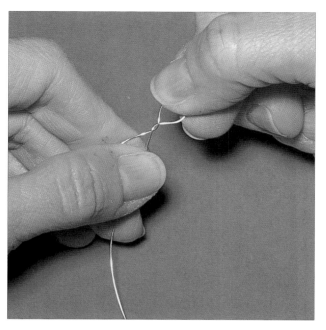

5. Take 46cm (18in) of wire and fold in half to find the middle, then make a loop. Twist twice to secure.

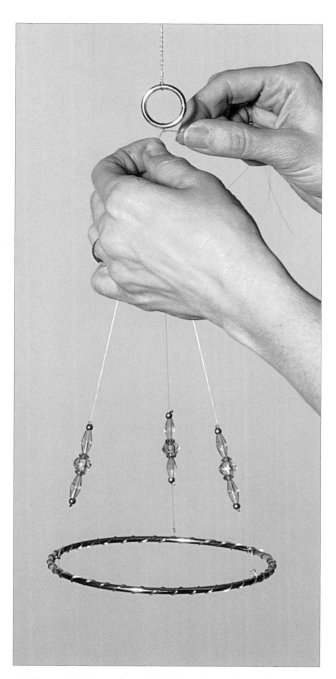

4. Thread all three beaded fishing lines through the 2.5cm (1in) metal ring and tie them so that the large metal ring hangs level, below the small ring.

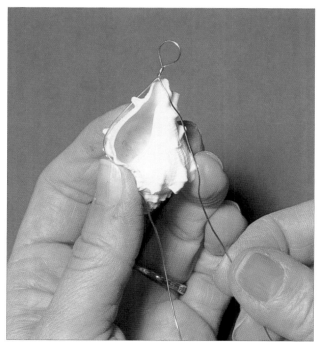

6. Place the loop at the tip of the open end of a shell, spreading the wires on opposite sides of the shell as shown.

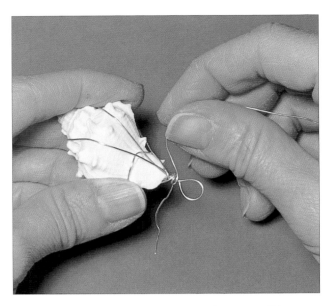

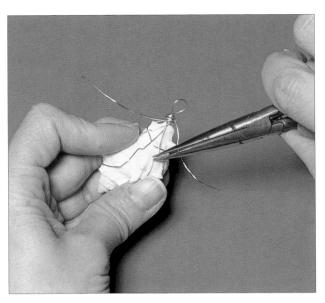

7. Wrap the wires around the shell, finishing off by wrapping around the base of the loop hanger. Leave about 4cm (1½in) at the ends of each wire.

8. Take long-nosed pliers and make little bends in the wire to hold it tighter against the uneven surface of the shell.

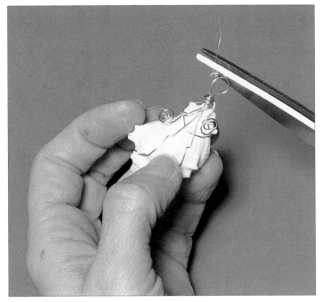

9. Make small coils with the two wire ends, starting with the round-nosed pliers and finishing by hand. Repeat steps 5–8 with a further fourteen shells.

10. Cut a 1m (39½in) piece of fishing line. Thread through a crimp bead, then thread through the loop on the shell, and back through the crimp bead. Secure by pinching with pliers and trim off the short end of the fishing line with scissors.

11. Thread a second crimp bead and secure by pinching in place about 7.5cm (3in) from the first crimp bead. Thread on the beads as shown. Secure in place by pinching a third crimp bead at the end of the bead pattern. Repeat steps 10 and 11 with the other fourteen decorated shells to make a total of fifteen chimes.

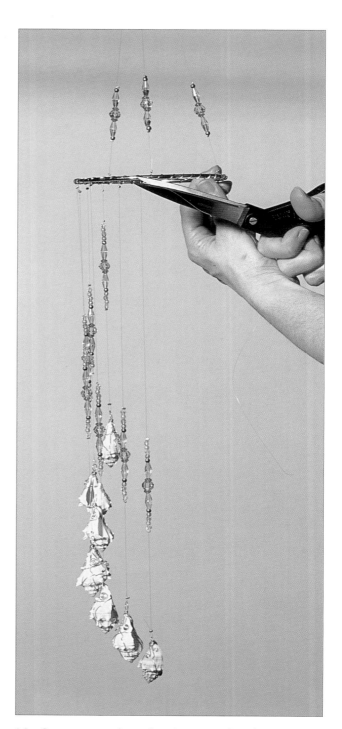

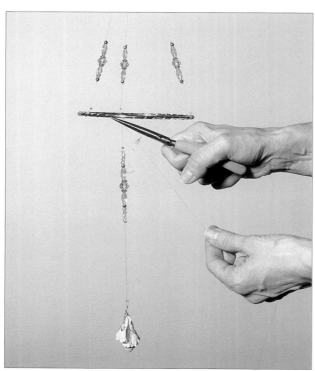

12. Take the chimes one at a time, and thread the fishing line around the hanging metal ring. Position the first one with the beads about 3cm (1¼in) down from the metal ring. Use a crimp bead to secure it in place. Snip off the excess fishing line with scissors.

13. Continue attaching the chimes so that they are about 2.5cm (1in) apart and each one hangs 2.5 cm (1in) longer than the previous one. Adjust the length according to the size of the shells, so that they overlap.

Graduating the chimes
so that each shell
hangs a little lower
than the previous one
creates a cascading
effect. It also ensures
that the shells tinkle
together when they are
touched by the breeze.

Decorated pots

Create unique elegance for the indoor garden with bead and wire trims on painted terracotta pots. It is amazing what effects you can create with a few simple techniques and modern acrylic paints. Add co-ordinating beads threaded between wire loops and curves and hung along the edge of the pot to create a stunning ornament in which to display your houseplants.

You will need

Terracotta pot

20 gauge copper coloured wire

Acrylic paint: black, dark green, light green, copper

Acrylic varnish

Beads:

14 x 10mm (^{5}/$_8$in x ^{3}/$_8$in) spiral oval antique copper

3mm (^{1}/$_8$in) round copper

4mm (^{1}/$_8$in) round matt black

Wire cutters

Long-nosed pliers

Round-nosed pliers

Ruler

Sponge brush

Natural sponge

1. Paint the pot with two coats of black acrylic paint, allowing it to dry completely between coats.

2. When the black paint is thoroughly dry, dampen a sponge and sponge the pot randomly with a dark green acrylic paint.

3. When dry, sponge the pot randomly with the light green paint.

4. When this is dry, highlight by sponging with copper metallic paint. Paint the pot with acrylic varnish.

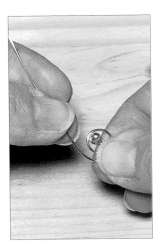

5. Take a 35cm (13¾in) length of copper wire. Thread on one 3mm copper bead and form a tight loop around the bead at one end of the wire, to hold it in place.

6. Using your fingers, form a loose coil around the copper bead.

7. Place the coil against the pot and use your fingers to bend the wire over the lip of the pot and down about 2cm (¾in) on the inside of the pot. Bend the wire and bring it back up over the lip of the pot.

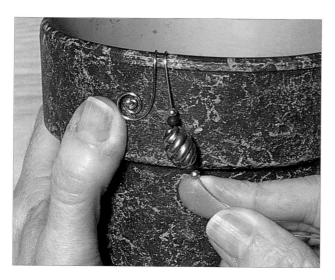

8. Thread a small copper bead, a small black bead, an antique copper bead, a second black bead and finally another small copper bead on to the wire.

9. Bring the wire down from the lip of the pot about 2cm (¾in) and form a curve large enough to take the five beads, then run the wire over the lip of the pot and back again as in step 7. Bring the copper wire down until it is level with the main bead cluster and trim the wire to 3.5cm (1¼in) longer than this.

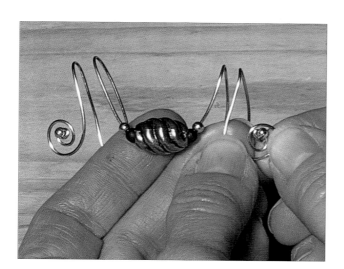

10. Finish by threading on a small copper bead and repeating steps 5 and 6.

11. Squeeze the wire into place against the pot. Make enough wire decorations to complete the top of the pot. You can pull some of the wire decorations higher in order to stagger them around the pot.

A verdigris paint effect with hints of copper provides the perfect backdrop for these antiqued metallised beads and copper wire coils.

Vary your choice of beads to
co-ordinate with different paint
effects, or with unpainted terracotta
for a natural look.

Christmas decoration

Combine beads and wire to create stylish Christmas tree ornaments. This project is a fir tree shape, but you can also make a bell or a cracker. Using the simple patterns on page 63, make wire forms which are then wired together to create the chosen three-dimensional design. Complete the look by decorating with beads for a stunning seasonal decoration.

You will need

18 gauge wire

24 gauge wire

38 round 6mm (¼in) pearl beads

Wire cutters

Long-nosed pliers

Round-nosed pliers

Ruler

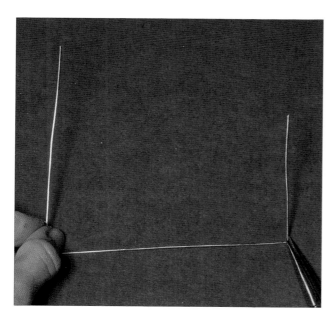

1. Cut a 28cm (11in) length of 18 gauge wire. Using long-nosed pliers, bend the wire at each end at right angles, one 10cm (4in) from the end and one 7cm (2¼in) from the other end. The middle stretch of wire should be 11cm (4¼in) long.

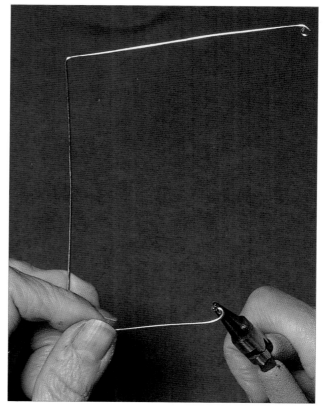

2. Using round-nosed pliers, form a small loop at both ends of the wire.

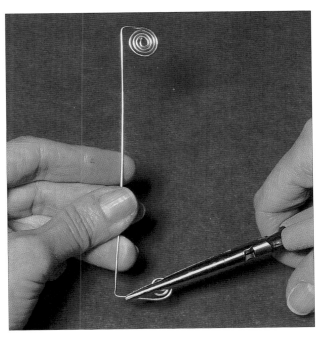

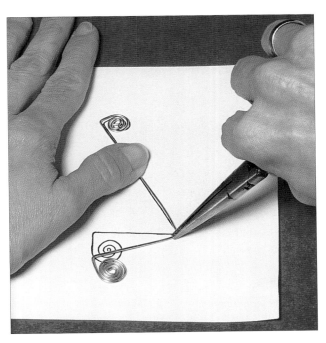

3. Change to long-nosed pliers and continue to work the wire round to form a tight coil at both ends.

4. Place the wire over the pattern on page 63 and bend as indicated, using long-nosed pliers.

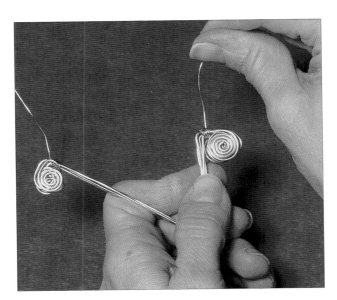

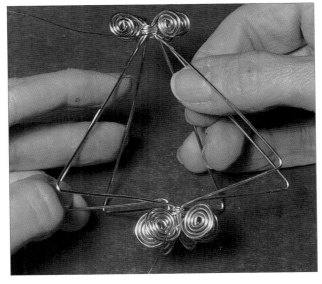

5. Make five more identical wire shapes and lay them on top of each other. Take two pieces of thin 24 gauge wire, one 51cm (20in), and one 122cm (48in) long. Secure the shapes together at the bottom and top respectively by wrapping the thin wire around them. Do not cut the long end of the wire.

6. Hold the shapes with the small coils uppermost. Spread the shapes out like the spokes of a wheel. Wrap the thin wire around the top of one of the shapes at the base of the coil.

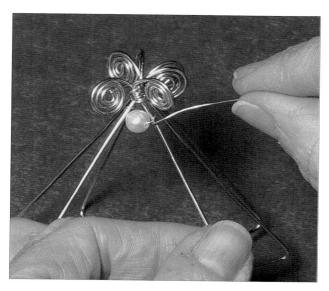

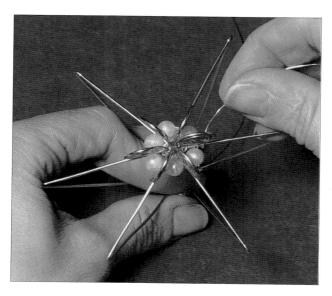

7. Thread a pearl bead on to the thin wire and wrap the wire around the next shape. This creates even spacing between the shapes.

8. Continue in this way around the top and bottom of the tree. Trim off the excess thin wire at the bottom of the tree. Do not cut the wire at the top of the tree.

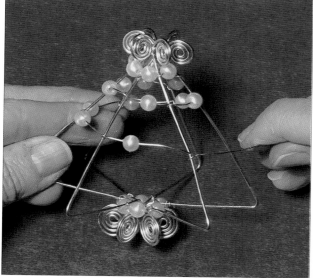

9. Take the thin wire at the top of the tree and wrap it once around one spoke of the tree. Thread on a bead and wrap the wire around the next spoke along, working at a slight downward angle. Thread another bead and wrap the wire around the next spoke along.

10. Continue in this fashion to the base of the tree, until there are 4 or 5 beads decorating each segment of the ornament.

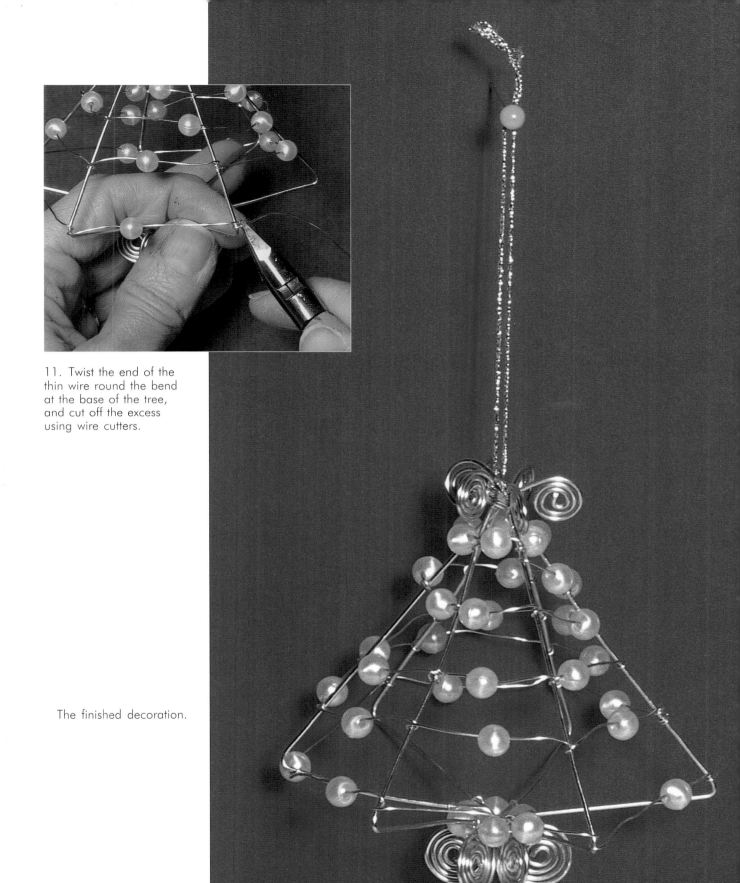

11. Twist the end of the thin wire round the bend at the base of the tree, and cut off the excess using wire cutters.

The finished decoration.

The tree, bell and Christmas cracker decorations shown here can be created using the patterns on page 63. The star shape is made using similar techniques. Blue and silver beads and wire, used in the bell decoration, create a very modern look.

Wedding goblets

Toast the bride and groom with these beautiful wedding goblets. Create delicate floral sprays with fine wire, leaf and flower beads, then attach them, along with ribbon, to stemmed glasses, using clear-drying silicone glue. We have used pearlised shades of ivory and green, but including the colours chosen for floral bouquets and bridesmaids' gowns can make your goblets the perfect finishing touch to the wedding day colour scheme.

You will need

Ribbon
24 gauge gold wire
Beads: Leaf
  Dogwood
  Starflower
  Baby's breath
  4mm ($\frac{1}{8}$in) round
  3mm ($\frac{1}{8}$in) round
Silicone glue
Wire cutters
Long-nosed pliers
Round-nosed pliers
Ruler

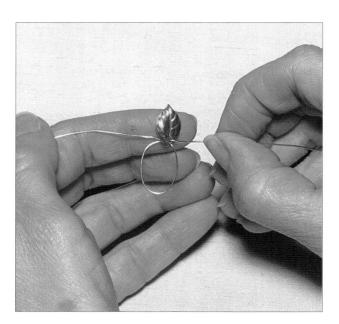

1. Cut 31cm (12in) of wire and string one leaf to the centre. Thread the wire through the hole in the leaf again, to stabilise the leaf.

2. Repeat with two more leaf beads to create a cluster.

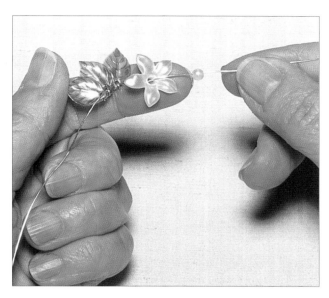

3. Using the longest wire, thread on a starflower and a small round pearl bead.

4. Thread the wire back through the starflower bead, securing the flower close to the leaf cluster.

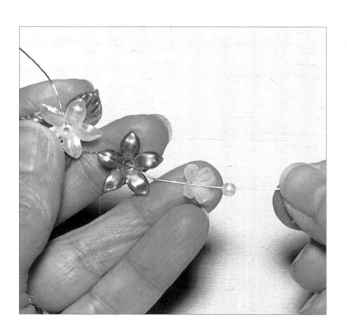

5. Thread a green starflower bead, followed by a dogwood flower bead and a 4mm round pearl bead.

6. Pass the wire back through the dogwood and green starflower beads.

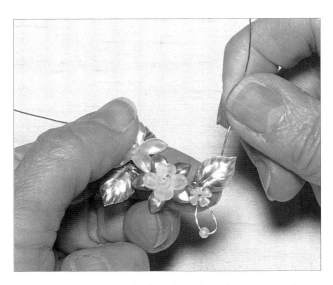

7. Next, thread on a leaf and re-thread as in step 2. Pass the wire through a small flower bead (baby's breath) and a 3mm round pearl bead. Thread the wire back through the baby's breath bead and secure to the leaf bead.

8. Trim both wire ends to about 5cm (2in). Make coils by forming a tight loop with the round-nosed pliers, then continuing to coil the wire using the long-nosed pliers.

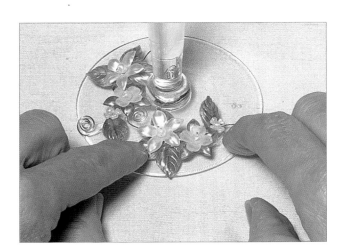

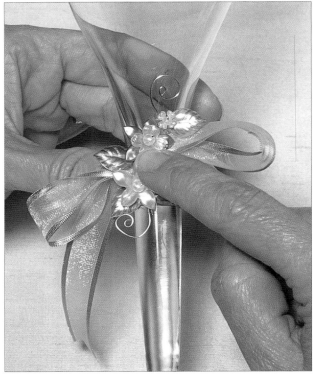

9. Make three more bead and wire sprays. Glue three sprays to the base of the glass using silicone glue.

10. Tie a bow around the top of the glass stem and stick the last bead and wire spray to the centre of the bow, using silicone glue.

The finished glass. Hand-decorated glasses like this can be adapted for different occasions by changing the colours of beads and ribbon.

The bead and wire floral sprays used for the wedding goblets can be used to create a whole range of wedding accessories. Attach them to photograph frames, handbags and other items using silicone glue or stitching.

Lampshade

Tiffany style lampshades with fringes of dangling beads have been popular for more than a century. The striking pattern of a repetitive scallop is no more difficult to make, yet adds a special style that sets it apart. In this project, looped braid provides the base to which the fringe is attached. The number of loops should be divisible by six, eight or ten (mine is divided by eight), and this can usually be achieved by stretching the braid to fit in the number of required loops while gluing it to the lampshade. Then simply make the different lengths of beaded wire and attach to the braid using jump rings.

You will need

Lampshade
Braid/gimp with loops
PVA glue
Hot glue gun (optional)
20 gauge gold wire
Beads: 4mm ($^1/_8$in) rose faceted
   crystal rondelles
   rose elongated bicone
   rose pendant, large and small

3mm ($^1/_8$in) round gold
Prong pendant bails
Gold jump rings
Wire cutters
Long-nosed pliers
Round-nosed pliers
Ruler
Measuring tape

1. Measure the bottom edge of the lampshade for the length of braid needed. Glue the braid round the lampshade, using PVA glue. Work out how many sets of eight beaded wires you need to fit your braid. You can also add braid to the top of the lampshade.

Note

A glue gun can be used to prevent braid from fraying. Before cutting, place a large drop of hot glue on the back of the braid, where you want to cut it. Let the glue cool for a few seconds, then press the braid down on to a smooth, burn-resistant surface such as a kitchen counter. This will spread the glue around the back and edges of the braid. When completely cool and dry, cut with sharp scissors.

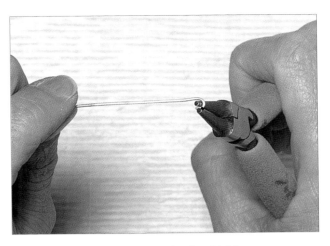

2. Take a 12.5cm (5in) length of gold 20 gauge wire. Using the round-nosed pliers, form a small loop at one end.

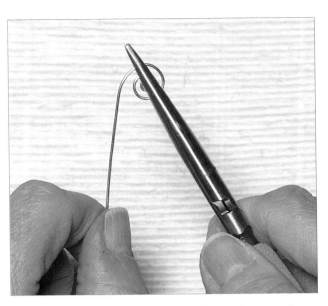

3. Take the long-nosed pliers and form a loose coil around the loop formed in step 2, using all but 7.5cm (3in) of wire.

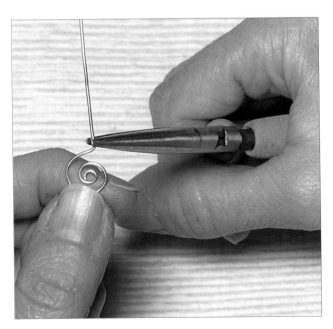

4. Using long-nosed pliers, bend the wire into a right angle at the base of the coil, to make an upside-down question mark shape.

5. Thread the beads as shown above. Trim off leaving 9mm (½in) of wire and complete the beaded wire with a small loop as shown in steps 1 and 2 of the bead link on page 12.

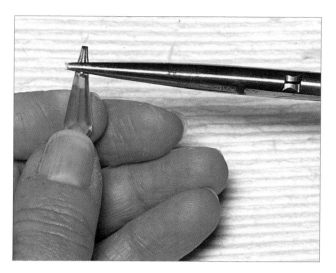

6. Take a small pendant bead and attach a prong pendant bail at the top. Use long-nosed pliers to squeeze the bail closed. This is the longest beaded wire and has a large pendant bead. The smaller beaded wires all use a small pendant bead. All the bead units use the same size prong pendant bail.

7. Open a jump ring and pass it through the bail at the top of the pendant, then attach it to the wire coil at the end of each beaded wire.

> **Note**
>
> To open a jump ring, twist it open, do not pull the sides apart.

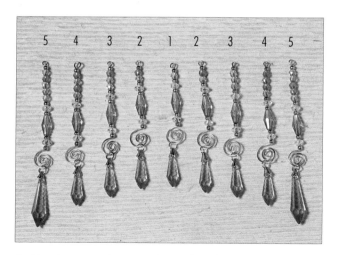

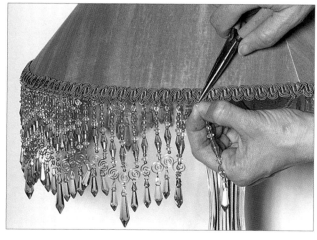

8. You have made a number 5 beaded wire, as shown above. Now make numbers 4, 3, 2, 1 and repeat 2, 3 and 4 to make a full set. (Number 5 is repeated here to show the full scalloped effect). Now make the required number of sets of eight, as worked out at step 1.

9. Open a jump ring and pass it through the loop at the top of a beaded wire, then attach it to a loop of the braid around the lampshade. Continue attaching the beaded wires in the order shown at step 8. Repeat this all the way round the lampshade.

The finished lampshade. This piece is particularly effective when the lamp is lit: the faceted transparent beads, gold coloured wire and small gold beads reflect the lamplight to give a rich glow.

Create a bold pattern of colour and texture by using smooth beads of different sizes. The matt finish on the beads used here forces the light to shine around rather than through them, making for more subdued lighting. For more movement when making long beaded wires, try making two or more wires, which are then attached to each other and hung from the braid.

Patterns

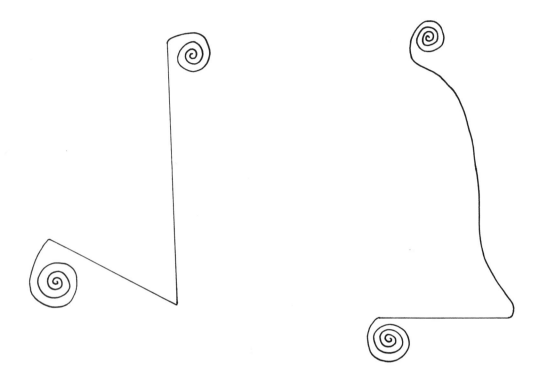

These patterns should be used as templates to help you bend the wire shapes needed to make the Christmas decorations shown on pages 46–51. Clockwise from top left, the patterns are for the fir tree decoration, the bell and the Christmas cracker.